Bible Promises
Warranty Guaranteed

Marylene Akakpo

Published in 2021 by Autumn House Publications (Europe) Ltd., Grantham, England.

British Library Cataloguing in Publication Data. A catalogue record for this book is available from the British Library.

Except where otherwise indicated, all Scripture quotations in this book are taken from the King James Version (KJV). Public Domain.

Other translations used:

The Holy Bible, English Standard Version, Anglicised (ESV). Copyright © 2001 by Crossway Bibles, a division of Good News Publishers.

The Holy Bible, New International Version®, Anglicised (NIV). Copyright © 1979, 1984, 2011 by Biblica, Inc. Used by permission. All rights reserved worldwide.

The Holy Bible, New King James Version® (NKJV). Copyright © 1982 by Thomas Nelson. Used by permission. All rights reserved.

The Holy Bible, New Revised Standard Version, Anglicised (NRSV). Copyright © 1989, 1995 by the Division of Christian Education of the National Council of the Churches of Christ in the United States of America. Used by permission. All rights reserved.

ISBN: 978-1-78665-929-3

Designed by the Stanborough Press design team.

Printed in India

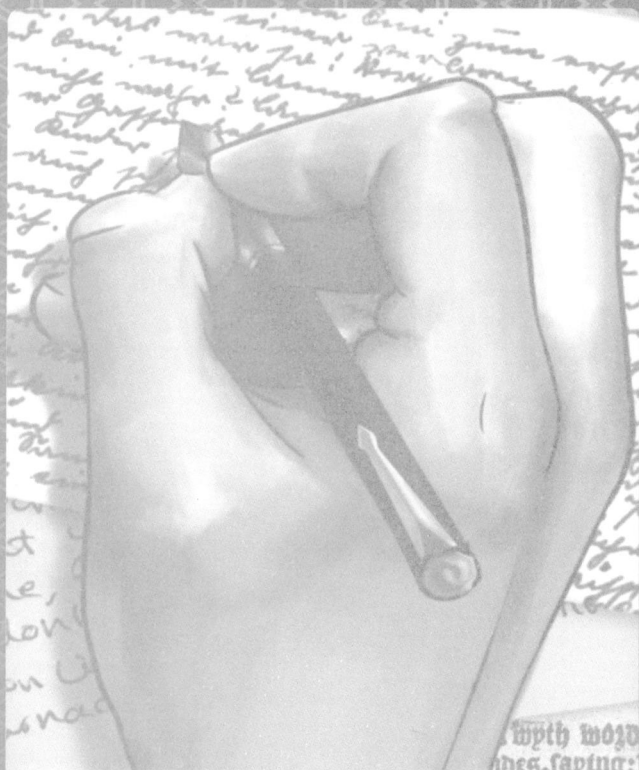

The Bible is God's love letter to mankind:
the most romantic, trustworthy and
powerful book in the world.

Table of Contents

About the author

Marylene is a shepherdess who loves the Lord, loves His Word and loves claiming the promises of God.

Her motto is: 'I can do all things through Christ which strengtheneth me' (Philippians 4:13).

Acknowledgements

I want to thank my daughter, Ashriah, for her help and support, and also Joy Alexander for her continuous encouragement and prayers.

I would also like to give special thanks to a very willing and creative young man, Liam Gallacher, who designed the original cover for this promise book. Even though he had a lot of coursework, he still made my cover his top priority, and for that I am genuinely grateful.

Finally, I want to thank the Lord for placing upon my heart the idea of putting together this little book of promises to help those who need encouragement.

The Bible

The Bible is the word of God. It is a collection of divine messages, messages that change lives and bring about inner peace and happiness. Psalm 119 sums it up beautifully in verse 11: 'Thy word have I hid in mine heart, that I might not sin against thee.' It gives strength, hope, wisdom, and sound counselling.

The Bible is God's love letter to mankind: the most romantic, trustworthy and powerful book in the world. It contains history, entertaining stories, and poetry. The Bible tells us who we are and where we come from. In the word of God there is life, health, love, and prosperity. In 3 John 2 the scripture says that God's wish for mankind is 'above all things that thou mayest prosper and be in health, even as thy soul prospereth'.

Every word that proceeds from the mouth of God is truth; for the scripture says, 'God is not a man, that He should lie' (Numbers 23:19, NKJV). Take time to read God's word for yourself and get acquainted with Him. Dig deep for its hidden treasure, and make the effort to secure it: 'For the word of God is quick, and powerful, and sharper than any twoedged sword, piercing even to the dividing asunder of soul and spirit, and of the joints and marrow, and is a discerner of the thoughts and intents of the heart' (Hebrews 4:12). It can both change and save lives.

One of my favourite writers, E. G. White, puts it this way: 'He whose heart is fixed to serve God will find opportunity to witness for Him. Difficulties will be powerless to hinder him who is determined to seek first the kingdom of God and His righteousness. In the strength gained by prayer and a study of the word, he will seek virtue and forsake vice. Looking to Jesus, the

Author and Finisher of the faith, who endured the contradiction of sinners against Himself, the believer will willingly brave contempt and derision. And help and grace sufficient for every circumstance are promised by Him whose word is truth. His everlasting arms encircle the soul that turns to Him for aid. In His care we may rest safely, saying, "What time I am afraid, I will trust in Thee." Psalm 56:3. To all who put their trust in Him, God will fulfil His **promise**' (*Acts of the Apostles*, p. 467, emphasis supplied).

Warranty guaranteed. Honour, obey, and love your BIBLE – Because It Brings Life Eternal.

The Word

Claiming the promise

Faith is yours to exercise if you believe. You must believe. God loves you; He wants to save you; and He wants to show you things that you know nothing about. Much faith is needed in our world today: faith that will cleave to God's wonderful promises.

God will never do for us what He has given us the power to do for ourselves, and that is to trust Him and to take Him at His word. This book, *Bible Promises: Warranty Guaranteed*, is here to encourage your faith and trust in God, and to guide you on how to claim His promises, as there are thousands of these promises in the word of God.

In the book of Daniel, chapter 6, it was Daniel's faith in God's word that shut the lions' mouths and preserved his life.

In Daniel chapter 3 it was faith in God's word that delivered the three Hebrew boys from the fiery furnace. They never got burnt; the fire had no power over them. Faith in the promises of God caused the children of Israel to go through the Red Sea on dry land, and by exercising faith in the promises of God's word you too can experience God's deliverance in your life.

'Faith is the substance of things hoped for' (Hebrews 11:1). In other words, faith is having complete trust or confidence in something, even though you have not yet received the thing or seen it with your eyes. Faith is like God saying, 'Take Me at My word.'

Now, this is an act of faith: we have never seen Jesus, yet we believe in Him; we also believe that He died and rose again. Can you see the picture? You believe it – right? In order to claim the promises of God, it is vitally important that you believe in His words: for 'all things are possible to him that believeth' (Mark 9:23).

In the Book of Genesis, God told Noah that it was going to rain, and by faith Noah built the ark as God instructed him to do, even though he had never seen rain before. God told Abraham to leave his father's house to go to a land that flows with milk and honey, a strange land. He did not have a clue where he was heading, yet by faith Abraham obeyed God and went in search of this land.

If, like Abraham, you were to be asked by God to do something impossible, would you act by faith on His word? Would you trust God? Would you have faith in Him, and would you take Him at His word? For when we take God at His word, we can never ever go wrong.

Now, you need to strengthen yourself by claiming the promises of God. He has never broken His promises. Numbers 23:19 tells us that God has the power to fulfil all of His promises, and Hebrews 4:12 also reminds us that the word of God is alive and well: it is still relevant for the twenty-first century. I am encouraging you today to search the Scriptures and find in them eternal life.

There are so many challenges in our world today. Whenever you feel lonely, alone, afraid, discouraged and in need of hope, read the word of God, and comfort your soul in the promises of His wonderful word. Do not neglect the salvation of your soul: claim the promises of God through prayer and the reading of God's word, and it will strengthen your heart in Him. Finally, never forget to thank Him.

Go through this book of promises, select a scripture that meets your needs, and then:

1. Reach out for your Bible and open it.
2. Confess your sins and ask God to forgive you for all your wrongs.
3. Place your finger on the promise in your Bible and claim it.
4. Open your heart to the Lord and ask Him to bless you.
5. Remember to always give God praise and thanks for answering your prayers.
6. End your prayers in Jesus' name.

John 14:6 tells us that Jesus is the way, the truth and the life, and that no man can come to the Father except through Him.

Ageing

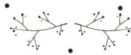

Psalm 46:1
'God is our refuge and strength,
a very present help in trouble.'

2 Corinthians 6:18 (NKJV)
'I will be a Father to you,
And you shall be My sons
and daughters,
Says the LORD Almighty.'

Isaiah 46:4 (ESV)
'Even to your old age I am he,
and to grey hairs I will carry you.
I have made, and I will bear;
I will carry and will save.'

Isaiah 40:31 (NKJV)

'But those who wait on the Lord
Shall renew their strength;
They shall mount up
with wings like eagles,
They shall run and not be weary,
They shall walk and not faint.'

Psalm 92:12-14

'The righteous shall flourish like the
palm tree: he shall grow like
a cedar in Lebanon. Those that be
planted in the house of the Lord shall
flourish in the courts of our God. They
shall still bring forth fruit in old age; they
shall be fat and flourishing.'

Psalm 84:11

'For the Lord God is a sun and shield:
the Lord will give grace and glory: no
good thing will he withhold from
them that walk uprightly.'

Isaiah 40:29

'He giveth power to the faint; and
to them that have no might he
increaseth strength.'

Isaiah 43:2 (ESV)

'When you pass through the waters, I
will be with you; and through the rivers,
they shall not overwhelm you; when
you walk through fire you shall not be
burned, and the flame shall
not consume you.'

Joshua 1:9 (NKJV)

'Have I not commanded you? Be strong
and of good courage; do not afraid, nor
be dismayed, for the LORD your God is
with you wherever you go.'

Deuteronomy 33:25

'Thy shoes shall be iron and brass; and
as thy days, so shall thy strength be.'

Psalm 73:26

'My flesh and my heart faileth: but God is the strength of my heart, and my portion for ever.'

2 Corinthians 4:16 (NKJV)

'Therefore we do not lose heart. Even though our outward man is perishing, yet the inward man is being renewed day by day.'

Psalm 37:25

'I have been young, and now am old; yet have I not seen the righteous forsaken, nor his seed begging bread.'

Afraid

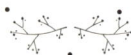

Isaiah 41:10 (ESV)

'Fear not, for I am with you;
be not dismayed, for I am your God;
I will strengthen you, I will
help you, I will uphold you with my
righteous right hand.'

Psalm 118:6, 7

'The LORD is on my side; I will not fear:
what can man do unto me? The LORD
taketh my part with them that help me.'

John 14:27

'Peace I leave with you, my peace I give unto you: not as the world giveth, give I unto you. Let not your heart be troubled,
neither let it be afraid.'

2 Timothy 1:7 (NKJV)

'For God has not given us a spirit of fear, but of power and of love and of a sound mind.'

Isaiah 43:1 (NKJV)

'But now, thus says the Lord, who created you, O Jacob,
And He who formed you, O Israel:
"Fear not, for I have redeemed you;
I have called you by your name;
You are Mine.'

Psalm 23:4

'Yea, though I walk through the valley of the shadow of death, I will fear no evil: for thou art with me; thy rod and thy staff they comfort me.'

Psalm 34:7 (ESV)

'The angel of the LORD encamps round those who fear him, and delivers them.'

Deuteronomy 31:6 (NIV)

'Be strong and courageous. Do not be afraid or terrified because of them, for the LORD your God goes with you; he will never leave you nor forsake you.'

Isaiah 41:13

'For I the LORD thy God will hold thy right hand, saying unto thee, Fear not; I will help thee.'

Confession

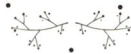

1 John 1:9

'If we confess our sins, he is faithful
and just to forgive us our sins, and to
cleanse us from all unrighteousness.'

Proverbs 28:13

'He that covereth his sins shall not
prosper: but whoso confesseth and
forsaketh them shall have mercy.'

1 John 2:1 (NRSV)

'My little children, I am writing these
things to you so that you may not sin.
But if anyone does sin, we have an

advocate with the Father, Jesus Christ the righteous.'

James 5:16 (NKJV)

'Confess your trespasses to one another, and pray for one another, that you may be healed. The effective, fervent prayer of a righteous man avails much.'

Psalm 51:7-11

'Purge me with hyssop, and I shall be clean: wash me, and I shall be whiter than snow. Make me to hear joy and gladness; that the bones which thou hast broken may rejoice. Hide thy face from my sins, and blot out all mine iniquities. Create in me a clean heart, O God; and renew a right spirit within me. Cast me not away from thy presence; and take not thy holy spirit from me.'

Psalm 103:8-12 (NKJV)

'The LORD is merciful and gracious,
Slow to anger, and abounding in mercy.
He will not always strive with us,
Nor will He keep His anger forever.
He has not dealt with us
according to our sins,
Nor punished us according
to our iniquities.
For as the heavens are high
above the earth,
So great is His mercy toward those
who fear Him;
As far as the east is from the west,
So far has He removed our
transgressions from us.'

2 Chronicles 7:14

'If my people, which are called by my
name, shall humble themselves, and
pray, and seek my face, and turn from
their wicked ways; then will I hear from
heaven, and will forgive their sin, and
will heal their land.'

Children

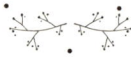

Ephesians 6:1-3 (NRSV)

'Children, obey your parents in the Lord, for this is right. "Honour your father and mother" – this is the first commandment with a promise: "so that it may be well with you and you may live long on the earth." '

2 Timothy 3:15 (NIV)

'And how from infancy you have known the Holy Scriptures, which are able to make you wise for salvation through faith in Christ Jesus.'

Matthew 19:14 (NKJV)

'But Jesus said, "Let the little children come to Me, and do not forbid them; for of such is the kingdom of heaven." '

1 Corinthians 16:13, 14 (NIV)

'Be on your guard; stand firm in the faith; be courageous; be strong. Do everything in love.'

Deuteronomy 5:16 (NRSV)

'Honour your father and your mother, as the LORD your God commanded you, so that your days may be long and that it may go well with you in the land that the LORD your God is giving you.'

John 14:15

'If ye love me, keep my commandments.'

Colossians 3:20 (ESV)

'Children, obey your parents in everything, for this pleases the Lord.'

Galatians 3:26

'For ye are all the children of God by faith in Christ Jesus.'

Matthew 5:9

'Blessed are the peacemakers: for they shall be called the children of God.'

Eternal life

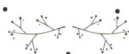

Proverbs 8:35 (NIV)

'For those who find me find life and receive favour from the Lord.'

1 John 5:11, 12 (NKJV)

'And this is the testimony: that God has given us eternal life, and this life is in His Son. He who has the Son has life; he who does not have the Son of God does not have life.'

John 10:10 (NIV)

'The thief comes only to steal and kill and destroy; I have come that they may have life, and have it to the full.'

John 6:35 (ESV)

'Jesus said to them, "I am the bread of life; whoever comes to me shall not hunger, and whoever believes in me shall never thirst." '

John 3:16

'For God so loved the world, that he gave his only begotten Son, that whosoever believeth in him should not perish, but have everlasting life.'

1 John 5:13

'These things have I written unto you that believe on the name of the Son of God; that ye may know that ye have eternal life, and that ye may believe on the name of the Son of God.'

John 17:3 (NRSV)

'And this is eternal life, that they may know you, the only true God, and Jesus Christ whom you have sent.'

John 14:6 (NIV)

'Jesus answered, "I am the way and the truth and the life. No-one comes to the Father except through me." '

John 6:40 (NKJV)

'And this is the will of Him who sent Me, that everyone who sees the Son and believes in Him may have everlasting life; and I will raise him up at the last day.'

John 10:27-29 (NKJV)

'My sheep hear My voice, and I know them, and they follow Me. And I give them eternal life, and they shall never perish; neither shall anyone snatch them out of My hand. My Father, who has given them to Me, is greater than all; and no one is able to snatch them out of My Father's hand.'

Psalm 139:23, 24

'Search me, O God, and know my heart: try me, and know my thoughts: And see if there be any wicked way in me, and lead me in the way everlasting.'

1 Timothy 6:12 (ESV)

'Fight the good fight of the faith. Take hold of the eternal life to which you were called and about which you made the good confession in the presence of many witnesses.'

Hebrews 7:25 (NKJV)

'Therefore He is also able to save to the uttermost those who come to God through Him, since He always lives to make intercession for them.'

Enemies

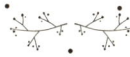

Romans 12:19, 20 (NRSV)

'Beloved, never avenge yourselves, but leave room for the wrath of God; for it is written, "Vengeance is mine, I will repay, says the Lord." No, "if your enemies are hungry, feed them; if they are thirsty, give them something to drink; for by doing this you will heap burning coals on their heads." '

Deuteronomy 28:7 (NIV)

'The Lord will grant that the enemies who rise up against you will be defeated before you. They will come at you from one direction but flee from you in seven.'

Psalm 35:1, 2

'Plead my cause, O Lᴏʀᴅ, with them that strive with me: fight against them that fight against me. Take hold of shield and buckler, and stand up for mine help.'

Isaiah 54:17 (NKJV)

' "No weapon formed
against you shall prosper,
And every tongue which
rises against you in judgment
You shall condemn.
This is the heritage of
the servants of the Lᴏʀᴅ,
And their righteousness is from Me,"
Says the Lᴏʀᴅ.'

Proverbs 16:7 (ESV)

'When a man's ways please the Lᴏʀᴅ, he makes even his enemies to be at peace with him.'

Deuteronomy 31:6

'Be strong and of a good courage, fear not, nor be afraid of them: for the LORD thy God, he it is that doth go with thee; he will not fail thee, nor forsake thee.'

Psalm 34:7, 8

'The angel of the LORD encampeth round about them that fear him, and delivereth them. O taste and see that the LORD is good: blessed is the man that trusteth in him.'

Psalm 31:15 (NKJV)

'My times are in Your hand;
Deliver me from the hand of my enemies,
And from those who persecute me.'

2 Kings 6:16

'And he answered, Fear not: for they that be with us are more than they that be with them.'

Psalm 138:7

'Though I walk in the midst of trouble, thou wilt revive me: thou shalt stretch forth thine hand against the wrath of mine enemies, and thy right hand shall save me.'

Encouragement

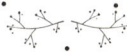

Isaiah 40:31

'But they that wait upon the Lord shall renew their strength; they shall mount up with wings as eagles; they shall run, and not be weary; and they shall walk, and not faint.'

Isaiah 43:2 (NKJV)

'When you pass through the waters, I will be with you;
And through the rivers, they shall not overflow you.
When you walk through the fire, you shall not be burned,
Nor shall the flame scorch you.'

Joshua 1:9

'Have not I commanded thee? Be strong and of a good courage; be not afraid, neither be thou dismayed: for the LORD thy God is with thee whithersoever thou goest.'

1 Corinthians 15:58

'Therefore, my beloved brethren, be ye stedfast, unmoveable, always abounding in the work of the Lord, forasmuch as ye know that your labour is not in vain in the Lord.'

Psalm 37:4

'Delight thyself also in the LORD; and he shall give thee the desires of thine heart.'

Mark 10:27 (NKJV)

'But Jesus looked at them and said, "With men it is impossible, but not with God; for with God all things are possible." '

Romans 8:28 (NKJV)

'And we know that all things work together for good to those who love God, to those who are the called according to His purpose.'

Philippians 4:13

'I can do all things through Christ which strengtheneth me.'

Forgiveness

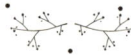

1 John 1:9 (NKJV)

'If we confess our sins, He is faithful and just to forgive us our sins and to cleanse us from all unrighteousness.'

2 Chronicles 7:14 (ESV)

'If my people who are called by my name humble themselves, and pray and seek my face and turn from their wicked ways, then I will hear from heaven and will forgive their sin and heal their land.'

Psalm 86:5 (NIV)

'You, Lord, are forgiving and good,
abounding in love to all who call to you.'

Matthew 6:14 (NRSV)

'For if you forgive others their
trespasses, your heavenly Father will
also forgive you.'

Luke 6:37

'Judge not, and ye shall not be judged:
condemn not, and ye shall not be
condemned: forgive, and ye shall
be forgiven.'

Isaiah 55:7

'Let the wicked forsake his way, and
the unrighteous man his thoughts: and
let him return unto the LORD, and he will
have mercy upon him; and to our God,
for he will abundantly pardon.'

Isaiah 1:18, 19

'Come now, and let us reason together, saith the Lord: though your sins be as scarlet, they shall be as white as snow; though they be red like crimson, they shall be as wool. If ye be willing and obedient, ye shall eat the good of the land . . .'

Micah 7:18, 19 (NKJV)

'Who is a God like You,
Pardoning iniquity
And passing over the transgression of the remnant of His heritage?
He does not retain His anger forever,
Because He delights in mercy.
He will again have compassion on us,
And will subdue our iniquities.
You will cast all our sins
Into the depths of the sea.'

Psalm 51:10, 11 (NRSV)

'Create in me a clean heart, O God, and put a new and right spirit within me. Do not cast me away from your presence, and do not take your holy spirit from me.'

Ephesians 4:31, 32

'Let all bitterness, and wrath, and anger, and clamour, and evil speaking, be put away from you, with all malice: And be ye kind one to another, tenderhearted, forgiving one another, even as God for Christ's sake hath forgiven you.'

Psalm 86:5 (ESV)

'For you, O Lord, are good and forgiving, abounding in steadfast love to all who call upon you.'

Faith

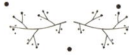

Matthew 21:22 (NRSV)

'Whatever you ask for in prayer with
faith, you will receive.'

Isaiah 26:3 (NKJV)

'You will keep him in perfect peace,
Whose mind is stayed on You,
Because he trusts in You.'

John 7:38 (NIV)

'Whoever believes in me, as Scripture
has said, rivers of living water will flow
from within them.'

Romans 15:13

'Now the God of hope fill you with all joy and peace in believing, that ye may abound in hope, through the power of the Holy Ghost.'

John 6:35

'And Jesus said unto them, I am the bread of life: he that cometh to me shall never hunger; and he that believeth on me shall never thirst.'

Hebrews 11:1

'Now faith is the substance of things hoped for, the evidence of things not seen.'

Hebrews 11:6

'But without faith it is impossible to please him: for he that cometh to God must believe that he is, and that he is a rewarder of them that diligently seek him.'

Luke 1:37

'For with God nothing shall
be impossible.'

Mark 16:16 (NIV)

'Whoever believes and is baptised will
be saved, but whoever does not believe
will be condemned.'

Matthew 21:21 (ESV)

'And Jesus answered them, "Truly, I
say to you, if you have faith and do not
doubt, you will not only do what has
been done to the fig tree, but even if
you say to this mountain, 'Be taken up
and thrown into the sea,' it will happen." '

James 1:5, 6

'If any of you lack wisdom, let him ask of
God, that giveth to all men liberally, and
upbraideth not; and it shall be given him.
But let him ask in faith, nothing

wavering. For he that wavereth is like a wave of the sea driven with the wind and tossed.'

Mark 11:24

'Therefore I say unto you, What things soever ye desire, when ye pray, believe that ye receive them, and ye shall have them.'

For singles

Genesis 2:18

'And the Lord God said, It is not good that the man should be alone; I will make him an help meet for him.'

Matthew 19:4, 5 (NKJV)

'And He answered and said to them, "Have you not read that He who made them at the beginning 'made them male and female,' and said, 'For this reason a man shall leave his father and mother and be joined to his wife, and the two shall become one flesh'?" '

2 Corinthians 6:14

'Be ye not unequally yoked together with unbelievers: for what fellowship hath righteousness with unrighteousness? and what communion hath light with darkness?'

Mark 11:24 (ESV)

'Therefore I tell you, whatever you ask in prayer, believe that you have received it, and it will be yours.'

Psalm 37:4

'Delight thyself also in the LORD; and he shall give thee the desires of thine heart.'

Ecclesiastes 4:9-11

'Two are better than one; because they have a good reward for their labour. For if they fall, the one will lift up his fellow: but woe to him that is alone when he falleth; for he hath not another to help him up. Again, if two lie together, then they have heat: but how can one be warm alone?'

1 Corinthians 7:1, 2
'It is good for a man not to touch a woman. Nevertheless, to avoid fornication, let every man have his own wife, and let every woman have her own husband.'

Isaiah 41:10 (NKJV)
'Fear not, for I am with you;
Be not dismayed, for I am your God.
I will strengthen you,
Yes, I will help you,
I will uphold you with My righteous right hand.'

Jeremiah 29:11 (NIV)
' "For I know the plans I have for you," declares the LORD, "plans to prosper you and not to harm you, plans to give you hope and a future." '

Isaiah 49:16 (ESV)

'Behold, I have engraved you on the palms of my hands; your walls are continually before me.'

Psalm 32:8 (NRSV)

'I will instruct you and teach you the way you should go; I will counsel you with my eye upon you.'

Single parents

Isaiah 49:25

'But thus saith the Lord, Even the captives of the mighty shall be taken away, and the prey of the terrible shall be delivered: for I will contend with him that contendeth with thee, and I will save thy children.'

Philippians 4:6 (NKJV)

'Be anxious for nothing, but in everything by prayer and supplication,

with thanksgiving, let your requests
be made known to God.'

2 Thessalonians 3:3

'But the Lord is faithful, who shall
stablish you, and keep you from evil.'

Matthew 6:33

'But seek ye first the kingdom of God,
and his righteousness; and all these
things shall be added unto you.'

Isaiah 58:11

'And the LORD shall guide thee
continually, and satisfy thy soul in
drought, and make fat thy bones: and
thou shalt be like a watered garden,
and like a spring of water, whose
waters fail not.'

Lonely singles

Matthew 6:33 (NRSV)

'But strive first for the kingdom of God and his righteousness, and all these things will be given to you as well.'

Philippians 4:19

'But my God shall supply all your need according to his riches in glory by Christ Jesus.'

Joshua 1:5

'There shall not any man be able to stand before thee all the days of thy life: as I was with Moses, so I will be with thee: I will not fail thee, nor forsake thee.'

1 Corinthians 7:9 (NIV)

'But if they cannot control themselves, they should marry, for it is better to marry than to burn with passion.'

Traits of a godly wife

1 Timothy 3:11 (NRSV)

'Women likewise must be serious, not slanderers, but temperate, faithful in all things.'

Proverbs 31:20

'She stretcheth out her hand to the poor; yea, she reacheth forth her hands to the needy.'

Proverbs 31:25, 26

'Strength and honour are her clothing; and she shall rejoice in time to come. She openeth her mouth with wisdom; and in her tongue is the law of kindness.'

Traits of a godly man

Honesty

Proverbs 12:22 (NKJV)

'Lying lips are an abomination to the Lord, But those who deal truthfully are His delight.'

Wisdom

Proverbs 13:20

'He that walketh with wise men shall be wise: but a companion of fools shall be destroyed.'

Humility

Luke 14:11 (ESV)

'For everyone who exalts himself will be humbled, and he who humbles himself will be exalted.'

Self-control

Proverbs 22:24

'Make no friendship with an angry man;
and with a furious man thou shalt
not go.'

Putting God first

1 Peter 1:15, 16 (NKJV)

'But as He who called you is holy,
you also be holy in all your conduct,
because it is written, "Be holy, for
I am holy." '

Financial blessings

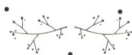

Malachi 3:10, 11 (NKJV)

' "Bring all the tithes into the storehouse,
That there may be food in My house,
And try Me now in this,"
Says the Lord of hosts,
"If I will not open for you
the windows of heaven
And pour out for you such blessing
That there will not be room enough
to receive it.
And I will rebuke the devourer for
your sakes,
So that he will not destroy the
fruit of your ground,

Nor shall the vine fail to bear fruit for
you in the field,"
Says the LORD of hosts.'

Deuteronomy 28:12 (ESV)

'The LORD will open to you his good
treasury, the heavens, to give the rain
to your land in its season and to bless
all the work of your hands. And you
shall lend to many nations, but you
shall not borrow.'

Philippians 4:19 (NIV)

'And my God will meet all your needs
according to the riches of his glory
in Christ Jesus.'

Isaiah 45:2, 3 (NRSV)

'I will go before you and level the
mountains, I will break in pieces the
doors of bronze and cut through the
bars of iron, I will give you the treasures
of darkness and riches hidden in secret
places, so you may know that it is I, the

Lᴏʀᴅ, the God of Israel, who call you by your name.'

Deuteronomy 8:18 (ESV)

'You shall remember the Lᴏʀᴅ your God, for it is he who gives you power to get wealth, that he may confirm his covenant that he swore to your fathers, as it is this day.'

Proverbs 19:17

'He that hath pity upon the poor lendeth unto the Lᴏʀᴅ; and that which he hath given will he pay him again.'

Jeremiah 29:11

'For I know the thoughts that I think toward you, saith the Lᴏʀᴅ, thoughts of peace, and not of evil, to give you an expected end.'

Grief

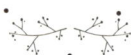

Psalm 34:18

'The LORD is nigh unto them that are of
a broken heart; and saveth such as be
of a contrite spirit.'

Matthew 5:4

'Blessed are they that mourn:
for they shall be comforted.'

1 Thessalonians 4:13, 14 (NIV)

'Brothers and sisters, we do not want
you to be uninformed about those
who sleep in death, so that you do not
grieve like the rest of mankind, who
have no hope. For we believe that

Jesus died and rose again, and so we believe that God will bring with Jesus those who have fallen asleep in him.'

Romans 8:38, 39

'For I am persuaded, that neither death, nor life, nor angels, nor principalities, nor powers, nor things present, nor things to come, nor height, nor depth, nor any other creature, shall be able to separate us from the love of God, which is in Christ Jesus our Lord.'

1 Thessalonians 4:16

'For the Lord himself shall descend from heaven with a shout, with the voice of the archangel, and with the trump of God: and the dead in Christ shall rise first.'

Isaiah 25:8 (NKJV)

'He will swallow up death forever, And the Lord God will wipe away tears from all faces;

The rebuke of His people
He will take away from all the earth;
For the Lᴏʀᴅ has spoken.'

2 Corinthians 1:3 (NKJV)

'Blessed be the God and Father of
our Lord Jesus Christ, the Father of
mercies and God of all comfort . . .'

1 Corinthians 15:52

'In a moment, in the twinkling of an eye,
at the last trump . . . the trumpet shall
sound, and the dead shall be raised
incorruptible, and we shall be changed.'

Isaiah 53:4

'Surely he hath borne our griefs, and
carried our sorrows: yet we did esteem
him stricken, smitten of God, and
afflicted.'

Psalm 147:3

'He healeth the broken in heart, and
bindeth up their wounds.'

1 Peter 5:7

'Casting all your care upon him;
for he careth for you.'

Health

3 John 2 (ESV)

'Beloved, I pray that all may go well
with you and that you may be in good
health, as it goes well with your soul.'

Proverbs 17:22

'A merry heart doeth good like a
medicine: but a broken spirit
drieth the bones.'

Proverbs 4:20-22 (NKJV)

'My son, give attention to my words;
Incline your ear to my sayings.
Do not let them depart from your eyes;
Keep them in the midst of your heart;

For they are life to those who find them,
And health to all their flesh.'

Isaiah 58:11 (NIV)

'The LORD will guide you always; he will satisfy your needs in a sun-scorched land and will strengthen your frame. You will be like a well-watered garden, like a spring whose waters never fail.'

Exodus 23:25 (NKJV)

'So you shall serve the LORD your God, and He will bless your bread and your water. And I will take sickness away from the midst of you.'

1 Corinthians 6:19, 20

'What? know ye not that your body is the temple of the Holy Ghost which is in you, which ye have of God, and ye are not your own? For ye are bought with a price: therefore glorify God in your body, and in your spirit, which are God's.'

Proverbs 3:7, 8

'Be not wise in thine own eyes: fear the
LORD, and depart from evil.
It shall be health to thy navel, and
marrow to thy bones.'

Proverbs 13:12

'Hope deferred maketh the heart sick:
but when the desire cometh,
it is a tree of life.'

Jeremiah 33:6

'Behold, I will bring it health and cure,
and I will cure them, and will reveal
unto them the abundance of peace
and truth.'

Exodus 15:26 (NRSV)

'He said, "If you will listen carefully to
the voice of the LORD your God, and do
what is right in his sight, and give heed
to his commandments and keep all his
statutes, I will not bring upon you any

of the diseases that I brought upon the Egyptians; for I am the L<small>ORD</small> who heals you." '

Proverbs 16:24

'Pleasant words are as an honeycomb, sweet to the soul, and health to the bones.'

1 Corinthians 10:31 (ESV)

'So, whether you eat or drink, or whatever you do, do all to the glory of God.'

Hope

Matthew 11:28

'Come unto me, all ye that labour and are heavy laden, and I will give you rest.'

Jeremiah 29:11 (NRSV)

'For surely I know the plans I have for you, says the Lord, plans for your welfare and not for harm, to give you a future with hope.'

Jeremiah 17:7 (NIV)

'Blessed is the one who trusts in the Lord, whose confidence is in him.'

Hebrews 11:1

'Now faith is the substance of things hoped for, the evidence of things not seen.'

Psalm 119:81

'My soul fainteth for thy salvation: but I hope in thy word.'

Psalm 119:114

'Thou art my hiding place and my shield: I hope in thy word.'

1 Peter 5:7 (NKJV)

'Casting all your care upon Him, for He cares for you.'

Philippians 1:6

'Being confident of this very thing, that he which hath begun a good work in you will perform it until the day of Jesus Christ.'

Love

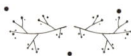

1 John 4:16

'And we have known and believed the love that God hath to us. God is love, and he that dwelleth in love dwelleth in God, and God in him.'

Jeremiah 31:3 (ESV)

'The LORD appeared to him from far away. I have loved you with an everlasting love; therefore I have continued my faithfulness to you.'

John 3:16 (NKJV)

'For God so loved the world that He gave His only begotten Son, that whoever believes in Him should not perish but have everlasting life.'

1 John 4:8

'He that loveth not knoweth not God; for God is love.'

John 14:21 (NKJV)

'He who has My commandments and keeps them, it is he who loves Me. And he who loves Me will be loved by My Father, and I will love him and manifest Myself to him.'

Romans 5:8

'But God commendeth his love toward us, in that, while we were yet sinners, Christ died for us.'

Romans 12:9, 10 (NRSV)

'Let love be genuine; hate what is evil, hold fast to what is good; love one another with mutual affection; outdo one another in showing honour.'

1 Peter 4:8 (NIV)

'Above all, love each other deeply, because love covers over a multitude of sins.'

John 15:9, 10

'As the Father hath loved me, so have I loved you: continue ye in my love. If ye keep my commandments, ye shall abide in my love; even as I have kept my Father's commandments, and abide in his love.'

Zephaniah 3:17 (ESV)

'The L<small>ORD</small> your God is in your midst, a mighty one who will save; he will rejoice over you with gladness; he will quiet you by his love; he will exult over you with loud singing.'

1 Peter 5:6, 7

'Humble yourselves therefore under the mighty hand of God, that he may exalt you in due time: casting all your care upon him; for he careth for you.'

Luke 6:27, 28 (NKJV)

'But I say to you who hear: Love your enemies, do good to those who hate you, bless those who curse you, and pray for those who spitefully use you.'

Marriage

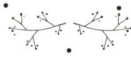

Working together as a team

Colossians 3:23

'And whatsoever ye do, do it heartily, as to the Lord, and not unto men.'

Philippians 1:9, 10

'And this I pray, that your love may abound yet more and more in knowledge and in all judgment; that ye may approve things that are excellent; that ye may be sincere and without offence till the day of Christ.'

Love endures all things

Ephesians 4:32

'And be ye kind one to another, tenderhearted, forgiving one another, even as God for Christ's sake hath forgiven you.'

Oneness

Proverbs 5:18

'Let thy fountain be blessed: and rejoice with the wife of thy youth.'

Romans 15:5, 6

'Now the God of patience and consolation grant you to be likeminded one toward another according to Christ Jesus: that ye may with one mind and one mouth glorify God, even the Father of our Lord Jesus Christ.'

Understanding & building your house on wisdom

Psalm 122:7

'Peace be within thy walls,
and prosperity within thy palaces.'

1 Peter 3:7 (NIV)

'Husbands, in the same way be
considerate as you live with your wives,
and treat them with respect as the
weaker partner and as heirs with you of
the gracious gift of life, so that nothing
will hinder your prayers.'

Proverbs 24:3, 4

'Through wisdom is an house builded;
and by understanding it is established:
and by knowledge shall the chambers
be filled with all precious and
pleasant riches.'

True love is loving each other as yourself

Ephesians 5:33

'Nevertheless let every one of you in particular so love his wife even as himself; and the wife see that she reverence her husband.'

Ephesians 5:22

'Wives, submit yourselves unto your own husbands, as unto the Lord.'

Ephesians 5:25

'Husbands, love your wives, even as Christ also loved the church, and gave himself for it.'

Colossians 3:19

'Husbands, love your wives, and be not bitter against them.'

When you need comforting

2 Corinthians 1:3, 4

'Blessed be God, even the Father of our Lord Jesus Christ, the Father of mercies, and the God of all comfort; who comforteth us in all our tribulation, that we may be able to comfort them which are in any trouble, by the comfort wherewith we ourselves are comforted of God.'

Asking God to bring husband or wife to repentance

2 Peter 3:9

'The Lord is not slack concerning his promise, as some men count slackness; but is longsuffering to us-ward, not willing that any should perish, but that all should come to repentance.'

Asking God to transform your spouse's heart and renew their mind that they may disern the will of God

Romans 12:2

'And be not conformed to this world: but be ye transformed by the renewing of your mind, that ye may prove what is that good, and acceptable, and perfect, will of God.'

Breaking up

1 Peter 5:7 (NKJV)

'Casting all your care upon Him, for He cares for you.'

John 14:27

'Peace I leave with you, my peace I give unto you: not as the world giveth, give I unto you. Let not your heart be troubled, neither let it be afraid.'

Psalm 34:18

'The LORD is nigh unto them that are of a broken heart; and saveth such as be of a contrite spirit.'

Isaiah 41:10

'Fear thou not; for I am with thee: be not dismayed; for I am thy God: I will strengthen thee; yea, I will help thee; yea, I will uphold thee with the right hand of my righteousness.'

Matthew 11:28-30

'Come unto me, all ye that labour and are heavy laden, and I will give you rest. Take my yoke upon you, and learn of me; for I am meek and lowly in heart: and ye shall find rest unto your souls. For my yoke is easy, and my burden is light.'

Obedience

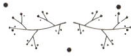

Jeremiah 7:23

'But this thing commanded I them,
saying, Obey my voice, and I will be
your God, and ye shall be my people:
and walk ye in all the ways that I have
commanded you, that it may be
well unto you.'

Deuteronomy 5:33

'Ye shall walk in all the ways which the
LORD your God hath commanded you,
that ye may live, and that it may be well
with you, and that ye may prolong your
days in the land which ye shall possess.'

Isaiah 1:19

'If ye be willing and obedient,
ye shall eat the good of the land.'

Exodus 19:5 (NKJV)

'Now therefore, if you will indeed obey
My voice and keep My covenant, then
you shall be a special treasure to
Me above all people; for all the
earth is Mine.'

Ephesians 6:1-3 (NIV)

'Children, obey your parents in the
Lord, for this is right. "Honour your
father and mother" – which is the first
commandment with a promise – "so
that it may go well with you and that
you may enjoy long life on the earth." '

Isaiah 1:19 (ESV)

'If you are willing and obedient, you
shall eat the good of the land.'

Deuteronomy 28:1, 2 (NKJV)

'Now it shall come to pass, if you diligently obey the voice of the Lord your God, to observe carefully all His commandments which I command you today, that the Lord your God will set you high above all nations of the earth. And all these blessings shall come upon you and overtake you, because you obey the voice of the Lord your God.'

Leviticus 18:5

'Ye shall therefore keep my statutes, and my judgments: which if a man do, he shall live in them: I am the Lord.'

1 Samuel 15:22

'Hath the Lord as great delight in burnt offerings and sacrifices, as in obeying the voice of the Lord? Behold, to obey is better than sacrifice, and to hearken than the fat of rams.'

Prayer

Philippians 4:6, 7 (NRSV)

'Do not worry about anything, but in everything by prayer and supplication with thanksgiving let your requests be made known to God. And the peace of God, which surpasses all understanding, will guard your hearts and your minds in Christ Jesus.'

1 Peter 4:7 (ESV)

'The end of all things is at hand; therefore be self-controlled and sober-minded for the sake of your prayers.'

James 5:16 (NIV)

'Confess your sins to each other and pray for each other so that you may be healed. The prayer of a righteous person is powerful and effective.'

Hebrews 4:16

'Let us therefore come boldly unto the throne of grace, that we may obtain mercy, and find grace to help in time of need.'

Luke 6:27, 28

'But I say unto you which hear, Love your enemies, do good to them which hate you, bless them that curse you, and pray for them which despitefully use you.'

Matthew 7:7, 8 (NIV)

'Ask and it will be given to you; seek and you will find; knock and the door will be opened to you. For everyone who asks receives; the one who seeks finds; and to the one who knocks, the door will be opened.'

1 John 2:1, 2 (NKJV)

'My little children, these things I write to you, so that you may not sin. And if anyone sins, we have an Advocate with the Father, Jesus Christ the righteous. And He Himself is the propitiation for our sins, and not for ours only but also for the whole world.'

1 John 5:14, 15

'And this is the confidence that we have in him, that, if we ask any thing according to his will, he heareth us: and if we know that he hear us, whatsoever we ask, we know that we have the petitions that we desired of him.'

Isaiah 65:24

'And it shall come to pass, that before they call, I will answer; and while they are yet speaking, I will hear.'

Jeremiah 33:3

'Call unto me, and I will answer thee, and shew thee great and mighty things, which thou knowest not.'

Mark 11:24 (ESV)

'Therefore I tell you, whatever you ask in prayer, believe that you have received it, and it will be yours.'

Hebrews 4:16

'Let us therefore come boldly unto the throne of grace, that we may obtain mercy, and find grace to help in time of need.'

Protection

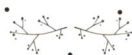

Ephesians 6:11

'Put on the whole armour of God, that ye may be able to stand against the wiles of the devil.'

Isaiah 54:17 (NIV)

' "No weapon forged against you will prevail, and you will refute every tongue that accuses you. This is the heritage of the servants of the Lord, and this is their vindication from me," declares the Lord.'

Exodus 14:14 (NRSV)

'The LORD will fight for you, and you have only to keep still.'

Psalm 91:4

'He shall cover thee with his feathers, and under his wings shalt thou trust: his truth shall be thy shield and buckler.'

Psalm 25:1, 2

'Unto thee, O LORD, do I lift up my soul. O my God, I trust in thee: let me not be ashamed, let not mine enemies triumph over me.'

Psalm 18:2

'The LORD is my rock, and my fortress, and my deliverer; my God, my strength, in whom I will trust; my buckler, and the horn of my salvation, and my high tower.'

Psalm 16:8 (NKJV)

'I have set the Lord always before me;
Because He is at my right hand I shall
not be moved.'

Psalm 46:1

'God is our refuge and strength,
a very present help in trouble.'

Parenting

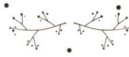

Proverbs 22:6

'Train up a child in the way he should go: and when he is old, he will not depart from it.'

Deuteronomy 6:6, 7 (NRSV)

'Keep these words that I am commanding you today in your heart. Recite them to your children and talk about them when you are at home and when you are away, when you lie down and when you rise.'

Proverbs 13:24

'He that spareth his rod hateth his son: but he that loveth him chasteneth him betimes.'

Jeremiah 31:16, 17 (NIV)

'This is what the Lord says: "Restrain your voice from weeping and your eyes from tears, for your work will be rewarded," declares the Lord.'

Matthew 19:14 (ESV)

'But Jesus said, "Let the little children come to me and do not hinder them, for to such belongs the kingdom of heaven." '

Proverbs 22:15

'Foolishness is bound in the heart of a child; but the rod of correction shall drive it far from him.'

Ephesians 6:4

'And, ye fathers, provoke not your children to wrath: but bring them up in the nurture and admonition of the Lord.'

Colossians 3:21

'Fathers, provoke not your children, lest they be discouraged.'

Isaiah 54:13

'And all thy children shall be taught of the LORD; and great shall be the peace of thy children.'

2 Timothy 3:16

'All scripture is given by inspiration of God, and is profitable for doctrine, for reproof, for correction, for instruction in righteousness.'

Proverbs 31:27, 28

'She looketh well to the ways of her household, and eateth not the bread of idleness. Her children arise up, and call her blessed; her husband also, and he praiseth her.'

Deuteronomy 4:9 (NKJV)

'Only take heed to yourself, and diligently keep yourself, lest you forget the things your eyes have seen, and lest they depart from your heart all the days of your life. And teach them to your children and your grandchildren.'

1 Chronicles 16:11

'Seek the LORD and his strength, seek his face continually.'

Hebrews 11:6 (NKJV)

'But without faith it is impossible to please Him, for he who comes to God must believe that He is, and that He is a rewarder of those who diligently seek Him.'

Peace

Galatians 5:22, 23

'But the fruit of the Spirit is love, joy, peace, longsuffering, gentleness, goodness, faith, meekness, temperance: against such there is no law.'

Matthew 5:9

'Blessed are the peacemakers: for they shall be called the children of God.'

John 14:27

'Peace I leave with you, my peace I give unto you: not as the world giveth, give I unto you. Let not your heart be troubled, neither let it be afraid.'

John 16:33

'These things I have spoken unto you, that in me ye might have peace. In the world ye shall have tribulation: but be of good cheer; I have overcome the world.'

Philippians 4:7

'And the peace of God, which passeth all understanding, shall guard your hearts and minds through Christ Jesus.'

Proverbs 16:7

'When a man's ways please the Lord, he maketh even his enemies to be at peace with him.'

Psalm 29:11

'The Lord will give strength unto his people; the Lord will bless his people with peace.'

Rest

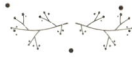

Matthew 11:28-30

'Come unto me, all ye that labour and are heavy laden, and I will give you rest. Take my yoke upon you, and learn of me; for I am meek and lowly in heart: and ye shall find rest unto your souls. For my yoke is easy, and my burden is light.'

Psalm 4:8

'I will both lay me down in peace, and sleep: for thou, LORD, only makest me dwell in safety.'

Genesis 2:2, 3 (NKJV)

'And on the seventh day God ended His work which He had done, and He rested on the seventh day from all His work which He had done. Then God blessed the seventh day and sanctified it, because in it He rested from all His work which God had created and made.'

Hebrews 4:9, 10 (NKJV)

'There remains therefore a rest for the people of God. For he who has entered His rest has himself also ceased from his works as God did from His.'

Exodus 20:8-11 (ESV)

'Remember the Sabbath day, to keep it holy. Six days you shall labour, and do all your work, but the seventh day is a Sabbath to the LORD your God. On it you shall not do any work, you, or your son, or your daughter, your male servant, or your female servant, or your livestock, or the sojourner who is within your gates. For in six days the LORD made heaven and earth, the sea, and all that is in them, and rested on the seventh day. Therefore the LORD blessed the Sabbath day and made it holy.'

Mark 2:27 (NIV)

'Then he said to them, "The Sabbath was made for man, not man for the Sabbath." '

Deuteronomy 5:12 (NIV)

'Observe the Sabbath day by keeping it holy, as the LORD your God has commanded you.'

Proverbs 1:33 (ESV)

'But whoever listens to me will dwell secure and will be at ease, without dread of disaster.'

Mark 2:28 (ESV)

'So the Son of Man is lord even
of the Sabbath.'

Sickness

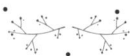

James 5:14, 15

'Is any sick among you? Let him call for the elders of the church; and let them pray over him, anointing him with oil in the name of the Lord. And the prayer of faith shall save the sick, and the Lord shall raise him up; and if he have committed sins, they shall be forgiven him.'

Exodus 23:25

'And ye shall serve the LORD your God, and he shall bless thy bread, and thy water; and I will take sickness away from the midst of thee.'

Deuteronomy 7:15

'And the LORD will take away from thee all sickness, and will put none of the evil diseases of Egypt, which thou knowest, upon thee; but will lay them upon all them that hate thee.'

James 5:15, 16 (NRSV)

'The prayer of faith will save the sick, and the Lord will raise them up; and anyone who has committed sins will be forgiven. Therefore confess your sins to one another, and pray for one another, so that you may be healed. The prayer of the righteous is powerful and effective.'

Psalm 41:3 (NKJV)

'The LORD will strengthen him on his bed of illness;
You will sustain him on his sickbed.'

Temptations

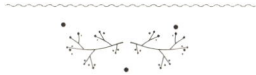

1 Corinthians 10:13 (ESV)

'No temptation has overtaken you that is not common to man. God is faithful, and he will not let you be tempted beyond your ability, but with the temptation he will also provide the way of escape, that you may be able to endure it.'

James 4:7

'Submit yourselves therefore to God. Resist the devil, and he will flee from you.'

Hebrews 2:18 (NKJV)

'For in that He Himself has suffered, being tempted, He is able to aid those who are tempted.'

1 Peter 5:8

'Be sober, be vigilant; because your adversary the devil, as a roaring lion, walketh about, seeking whom he may devour.'

Ephesians 6:11

'Put on the whole armour of God, that ye may be able to stand against the wiles of the devil.'

Trust

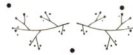

Proverbs 3:5, 6

'Trust in the Lord with all thine heart; and lean not unto thine own understanding. In all thy ways acknowledge him, and he shall direct thy paths.'

Psalm 125:1

'They that trust in the Lord shall be as mount Zion, which cannot be removed, but abideth for ever.'

Isaiah 26:3 (NIV)

'You will keep in perfect peace those
whose minds are steadfast,
because they trust in you.'

Psalm 91:1, 2 (NRSV)

'You who live in the shelter of the Most
High, who abide in the shadow of the
Almighty, will say to the LORD, "My
refuge and my fortress; my God, in
whom I trust." '

Psalm 37:5, 6 (NKJV)

'Commit your way to the LORD,
Trust also in Him,
And He shall bring it to pass.
He shall bring forth your righteousness
as the light,
And your justice as the noonday.'

Psalm 9:10

'And they that know thy name will put
their trust in thee: for thou, Lord, hast
not forsaken them that seek thee.'

Proverbs 30:5

'Every word of God is pure:
he is a shield unto them that put their
trust in him.'

Psalm 62:8 (NKJV)

'Trust in Him at all times, you people;
Pour out your heart before Him;
God is a refuge for us.'

Wisdom

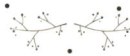

James 1:5 (NIV)

'If any of you lacks wisdom, you should ask God, who gives generously to all without finding fault, and it will be given to you.'

Psalm 111:10

'The fear of the Lord is the beginning of wisdom: a good understanding have all they that do his commandments: his praise endureth for ever.'

Proverbs 2:7, 8

'He layeth up sound wisdom for the righteous: he is a buckler to them that walk uprightly. He keepeth the paths of judgment, and preserveth the way of his saints.'

Proverbs 4:8 (NIV)

'Cherish her, and she will exalt you; embrace her, and she will honour you.'

James 3:17

'But the wisdom that is from above is first pure, then peaceable, gentle, and easy to be entreated, full of mercy and good fruits, without partiality, and without hypocrisy.'

Colossians 4:5, 6 (NRSV)

'Conduct yourselves wisely towards outsiders, making the most of the time. Let your speech always be gracious,

seasoned with salt, so that you
may know how you ought to
answer everyone.'

James 3:13 (NKJV)
'Who is wise and understanding
among you? Let him show by good
conduct that his works are done in the
meekness of wisdom.'

Proverbs 19:20 (NIV)
'Listen to advice and accept discipline,
and at the end you will be counted
among the wise.'

Youth

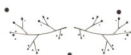

1 Timothy 4:12 (NRSV)

'Let no one despise your youth, but set the believers an example in speech and conduct, in love, in faith, in purity.'

Ephesians 6:1-3

'Children, obey your parents in the Lord: for this is right. Honour thy father and mother; (which is the first commandment with promise;) that it may be well with thee, and thou mayest live long on the earth.'

Proverbs 1:8, 9

'My son, hear the instruction of thy father, and forsake not the law of thy mother: for they shall be an ornament of grace unto thy head, and chains about thy neck.'

Ecclesiastes 12:1

'Remember now thy Creator in the days of thy youth, while the evil days come not, nor the years draw nigh, when thou shalt say, I have no pleasure in them.'

Deuteronomy 31:6

'Be strong and of a good courage, fear not, nor be afraid of them: for the Lord thy God, he it is that doth go with thee; he will not fail thee, nor forsake thee.'

Proverbs 23:22 (NIV)

'Listen to your father, who gave you life, and do not despise your mother when she is old.'

Proverbs 3:5, 6 (ESV)

'Trust in the LORD with all your heart, and do not lean on your own understanding.
In all your ways acknowledge him, and he will make straight your paths.'

John 16:24 (NKJV)

'Until now you have asked nothing in My name. Ask, and you will receive, that your joy may be full.'

Romans 15:13 (NRSV)

'May the God of hope fill you with all joy and peace in believing, so that you may abound in hope by the power of the Holy Spirit.'

Joshua 1:9 (NKJV)

'Have I not commanded you? Be strong and of good courage; do not be afraid, nor be dismayed, for the LORD your God is with you wherever you go.'

Mark 12:29-31 (NIV)

' "The most important one," answered Jesus, "is this: 'Hear, O Israel: the Lord our God, the Lord is one. Love the Lord your God with all your heart and with all your soul and with all your mind and with all your strength.' The second is this: 'Love your neighbour as yourself.' There is no commandment greater than these." '